An Amateur's Guide to

READY GOLF

How to play in four hours or less.

By

Doug Farnsworth

Picture on the cover was courtesy of Mountain Brook Golf Club, Gold Canyon, AZ

Table of Contents

Dedication

I don't know if anyone really reads the Dedications in books. I don't generally. But this is my first book, and I feel it is warranted. My thanks and praise be to God for the opportunity to play the great game of golf. Doing so has given me a greater appreciation for His creation.

Special thanks to my father, who introduced me to the game and instilled in me the passion to play it to the best of my ability. He knew this crazy game would teach me persistence, self-control, and humility.

Thanks to the people I have played with in the past and today who continue to put up with me. And lastly, I thank the thousands of golfers that are the driving force behind this book.

About the Author

I'm nothing special to the golf world. I am not a professional golfer, ex-professional golfer, teaching professional or semi-professional. For that matter, I am just an amateur like you. I'm not much of a writer either, but I'll try.

I started playing the game at age 12, thanks to my father. He wasn't much of a golfer. He was more of a weekend hacker, but he loved the game. He taught me to do the same. And I do love the game to this day in my 70's.

I grew up in Indiana, where our golf season was limited. We got to play golf for about five months of the year (weather permitting). When I was young, my friends and I rode our bikes nine miles to a 9-hole course just across the Indiana/Ohio state line to play. We would play three to four rounds and be sure to ride home before dinner. There was always this one house we passed that had a dog with an attitude. We learned to get up speed so we could coast by with our feet up on the bike frame away from this maneater.

It was at this course I bought my first set of golf clubs. Northwestern. I was able to do this from my paper route money. I played with that set until I turned 16. My next set was by Tony Penna. The woods were persimmon. I still have those in the attic.

I would imagine starting to play so young is what led me to the high school golf team. Since we only had 200 in the entire high school, I didn't have to be very good to make the team. My brother was on the team, too. He was much better.

Our golf coach was also the baseball coach, freshman basketball coach, driver training instructor, and history teacher. He approached all of these without a great deal of focus. That explains why I never had a golf lesson or was taught any fundamentals of the game.

I recall playing in the state sectional golf championship in my junior year of high school. I was listed as a "#4" player on a five-man team. That means the three others on the team were better than me, and only one not. In the tournament, two #4's were paired with two #1's. Each was from a different high school. We played at the Brookwood GC in Fort Wayne, IN. That was the same course where I played my very first round.

The reason I mention this is one of the #1's I played against would eventually join the PGA tour and later become a national broadcaster. He was the medalist of the Sectional tournament that year with a 9-hole score of 35. I am sure he would not care to admit some of his on-course antics that year. He was young and had anger issues. I won't go into details. At any rate, I shot my usual 44. Not terrible, but not stellar either.

I continued to play golf in college, but only recreationally. I was not even close to being "team material". I was lucky enough to date a girl whose father owned a golf course. The free play made golf possible for this "starving student". My game got better, and I had a ton of fun. I was even shooting in the high 70's low 80's.

Once I graduated and began working for a living, my golf game suffered. My play became weekends only and eventually to only a couple times a month. Yes, back to the high 80's and then 90's. It wasn't long after marriage and children (in my late 30's and 40's) that golf became more of an afterthought. It seemed the closest I could get to a course was television. (More about that later) If you have a family, you know what I mean. I can even recall going a full year and only playing three times. Boy, does that play havoc with your short game! Back to bogey golf as a goal.

In my late 40's and then 50's, I decided to take lessons. That got me back on track. I was then playing Ping irons and Cobra woods. During that time, I was also lucky enough to avail myself of business golf. I got to play some of the nation's best courses, like Doral, Baltusrol, TPC Sawgrass, Colonial, Robert Trent Jones Golf Trail, Calloway Gardens, etc. I even was fortunate to play the "Old Course" at Saint Andrews.

Now in my 70's and somewhat "retired", I find myself playing more frequently. I even got "fitted" for irons for the first time in my life. I'm now playing Calloway Rogue irons. Still have my cobra woods. Replaced the stiff shafts with regulars. I replaced the long irons with hybrids. Getting older causes a loss of distance.

Long gone are those days when I could hit the ball like young "long-haired limber backs".

Being the Starter at an Arizona golf club makes it possible to play more. I'm still not very good at the game, but I love it just as much as I did as a kid. In that regard, I may never grow up.

Introduction

I was told I had to have an Introduction to the book. I never read these. I just jump into the book and look for some pearls of wisdom. Oh well, guess I need to do this., so here goes.

As you know (if you read "About the Author"), I am a Starter at an Arizona golf club. In this position, I see a couple of hundred golfers a day. No two are the same, and most never took a lesson in their life. Or maybe they did but it didn't take. This book offers you an inside look at today's typical golfer. That's a person that sincerely believes he is on the verge of breaking par if only……..

The course I work at is local to many senior communities. The members play almost every day. They generally play from the forward tees and make use of the "breakfast ball". That's another term for a Mulligan to those of you back East.

According to the experts, the average golfer nationwide struggles to break 100. I think that includes many weekend and vacation golfers. We have our share of those here as well.

I get very frustrated with the multitude of players who make this great game miserable for themselves and others. We have all heard the saying, "Golf is a game you love to hate". I now know what is behind the saying. I see it every day.

I saw this the other day. It is very apropos.

"You have fits of rage, followed by
temporary spells of euphoria, all within
several hours. Are you, by chance, a
golfer?"

I get weary of folks complaining about slow play. Often, they themselves are slow. I can only assume the people who play a 4 ½ hour to 5-hour round do not know how to play, or they just don't want to go home.

Our course puts the suggested length of play for each hole. The time for a round should be 4 hours. Unfortunately, it isn't taken to heart by many. The Ranger/Marshall is kept busy.

One course in New Zealand posted the following sign to address slow play.

This needs to be posted at every course. However, most golfers do not know what 4. **Ready Golf** means.

I am writing this book in an attempt to change that. Teaching people how to play "**Ready Golf**" can get them to that goal of a 4-hour round.

I promise to keep the book short and to the point. I don't read often, either. I don't usually take the time. Mine is valuable. I believe yours is as well.

When you are done reading this, buy an extra copy for the group in front of you. Just be sure to carry your 7-iron in the event they don't appreciate the gift.

Chapter 1 - Preparation

Believe it or not…. preparing to play the evening (day) before your round may actually improve your game. I have seen people show up to the course without their golf shoes. I have even seen some riding in on their own carts without their clubs.

There have been others that went to the wrong course or had the wrong day or the wrong tee time. All of these are too normal and may cause you stress, embarrassment, anger, or frustration.

That does not even begin to describe what it does to your playing partners, the group scheduled right after you, and, yes, the Starter.

Lack of preparation will adversely impact your game. To avoid problems like these, you should:

- Locate your golf clubs and put them in an accessible spot.

- Put your shoes with your clubs.

- Be sure your range finder is charged and with your clubs.

- Check the weather and decide what you will wear and lay out your clothes.

- Double check and verify the course you are playing and the tee time you have.

- Confirm travel arrangements ahead of time. Don't wait until an hour before your tee time to ask your buddies for a ride.

This may sound a bit too organized for you, but the way you play is often a reflection of how well you prepare.

Chapter 2 - Game Day –
Before You Begin Play

Make arrangements to arrive at the course in sufficient time to drop off clubs, park, get your shoes on, register in the Pro Shop, hit balls if you choose, and still be at the 1st tee no less than 5 minutes before your scheduled tee time. This is a key component of **Ready Golf.**

I have seen players wait until they get to the first tee to put on their shoes or do stretching exercises. This disrespects everyone around them.

Why 5 minutes? Often, courses are running ahead. Sometimes, groups ahead of you cancel at the last minute. This allows you the opportunity to play without being rushed before the next group is due on the tee.

Let's go back to the topic of hitting balls. Some golfers insist on warming up on the range by hitting balls. Golfers who play frequently generally get the smaller amount of range balls offered, while those who play rarely choose larger amounts of range balls.

Regardless of which you choose, give yourself enough time ahead of your scheduled tee time to do the warmup you want. Don't rely on the loudspeaker system to remind you. Having the course outside staff come get you on the range isn't cool.

Speaking of the driving range…..If you are someone playing golf for the first or second time, do not attempt to play on a regulation course, especially during peak times. An 18 hole course is not the place to start playing the game. It will destroy your morale and the game of everyone else on the course at the time.

Beginners should make several trips to the practice range and acquire capable instruction before even attempting to play on a regulation course. You should probably play an executive (par 3) course first.

Experienced golfers that have a novice spouse or friend should know that. Do everyone a favor and do your instruction on the range. I have seen people give impromptu lessons on the course only to cause huge back-ups, lengthy delays, and fits of "fairway rage".

I also have a suggestion for playing with a novice spouse, child, or friend. Play a two-man scramble. Both hit from the same spot. Then pick-up the poorer shot and move it to where the better shot lies. Both hit the next shots from there. This way, they won't get frustrated and can enjoy a round of golf. No one behind you will get annoyed, either.

Speaking of lessons….. I waited much too long in life to avail myself of this tool. It's so easy to see what someone else is doing to hurt their game. Yet it is almost impossible to see what you are doing to hurt yours. We all have a tendency to think the problem is our equipment.

I recall a teaching pro listening to me complain that one of my problems was my outdated driver. He proceeded to take it from me and hit the ball over 300 yards. Duh!

I saw this cartoon the other day and thought how true it is of the average golfer.

Game Break: Don't spend your money on a new driver or clubs until you take a few lessons from a teaching pro. You will be amazed at how much it will help your game and your enjoyment of it.

Back to pre-game.

Another key component of **Ready Golf** is taking care of the pre-game haggling that may be involved in your group. Get this out of the way before you get on the tee-box. It really irks me to have a foursome on the 1st tee arguing what the bet of the day is or who is getting how many strokes and on what holes. Everything needs to be decided before you go to the tee.

On the tee is not time to decide who goes first. No time to start flipping tees. Who cares? What difference does it make? There are no "honors" on the first tee. Last weekend, I saw a twosome flip a tee to see who would hit first. This is insane! If you must decide, do it before you get to the tee.

The same goes for what tee to play….black, blue, white, gold, red. Decide this before you walk onto the tee box. Another way to speed play is for all members of the group to play from the same tees. I realize that is not always possible, but it will help when you do.

Too often, I see golfers playing from the back tees (the "tips") when they can barely reach the forward tees. More often than not, it is the male golfer in their 20's or 30's. They must think playing from anything other than the back tees means they are weak.

I have seen many start their game angry or embarrassed. They swing so hard they miss the ball, top the ball, or hit it OB. Why? Play the tees you are capable of playing. This isn't a game of who can hit the ball farther. It is one of accuracy and scoring.

I strongly suggest that anyone with a handicap of 15 or higher use white tees. It will cause less player frustration and speed up the game. Give yourself a chance to beat bogey golf.

There may be times when you do not have a foursome booked. The course may, at its discretion, put other players with you. When this happens, introduce yourself. Do this before you get to the tee. Don't delay on the tee getting to know them, where they are from, how long they have been in the area, etc. Find out what tees everyone is playing. If possible, play from the same tees.

Lastly, familiarize yourself with the pace of play designated by that course. Many courses now have pace of play printed on the scorecards. Some have it hole by hole. If it is not there, ask the Starter. Then follow it.

You will never be reprimanded or cautioned by the Ranger (Marshall) if you keep pace with the group ahead of you.

Chapter 3 - #1 Tee

You have now arrived at the first tee with wagers finalized. You have done your warmup. Your club of choice is in hand. Your group has already told each other what ball they're playing. The starter has given you the go sign.

The rule of thumb is for the shorter hitters to go first. This practice speeds play. Longer hitters should not be the first to hit. Then they don't have to stand there holding up everyone waiting for the fairway to clear. This is especially true if members of your group are playing from different tees and the tees are not far apart.

Players should never sit in the cart waiting for their turn to hit. They should be on the tee with a ball in hand, standing behind the player that is hitting.

Another thing that slows play is the "Mulligan". This is often referred to in Senior circles as the "breakfast ball". Funny how breakfast can now be served all day. This "extra" ball can bring play to a halt, especially when the person using it did not bring a second ball with him/her and must go back to the cart for one. I just shake my head and watch groups that are waiting moan and groan. More than half of the time, the second ball is not better and even worse than the first. That happens when the golfer rushes to hit the second ball, trying to avoid embarrassment.

As a Starter, I have told groups there can be no Mulligans if the group comes to the tee late or we are running late due to slow play. I know you may say that isn't fair, but I see no cotton candy or Ferris wheels.

I also firmly believe no league should allow extra balls at any time. It slows play. Leave those Mulligans for the charity event donations. I do admit it is difficult to stop Mulligans when the golfer is paying over $100 to play. Just be quick about it, and if your group allows it, have a ball in your pocket when you go to the tee.

Too often I see golfers waiting and waiting for someone 280 yards out in the fairway to clear. They can't hit it that far. If they could, they should be playing the back tee or be on tour. Too many golfers think they can hit the ball like a pro. Those guys usually spray the ball left or right. Some don't even make it to the forward tees. I've seen it all.

I know some golfers can launch the ball. They should defer to the shorter hitters on the tee and take out their cannons last. If your entire group are gorillas, tell the starter. He/she will increase the time spread from the previous group.

Remember, the Starter's job is to get golfers on the course at or before their scheduled time and with enough gap between groups that no one is delayed from the prescribed pace of play. After the first tee, it becomes the Ranger's job.

Allow me to address another component of slow play. Today's golfers watch too much golf on television. They believe they must stand behind the ball for several seconds with their club outstretched in front of them, staring down the wide-open fairway.

I have even seen golfers stand behind the ball. Then, take their stance and make a practice swing or two. Then, go back behind the ball again and look down the fairway. Why? The view has not changed! It is even more ridiculous when the golfer is playing their home course.

Some golfers have perfected the so-called waggle into an art form. Wasn't that deemed out of fashion a decade ago? Just the other day I actually saw a golfer practice the pose. At the end of his practice swing, he stood there as if to admire his "virtual" shot as it soared down the middle of the fairway. I thought I had seen it all.

The majority of golfers I see never swing at the ball with the same motion as their practice swings. Some aren't even close. So why take several swings? Do your swings on the practice range.

Then there is the guy who takes several practice swings and then stands over the ball like a statue. I have counted to ten seconds in one case before he took the swing. I heard from fellow golfers he does that over every shot. Many choose not to play with him. I can understand why. Who wants a 5-hour round? It reminds me of Sergio's multiple regrips. Everyone is thinking, "Pull the trigger already!"

This brings me to another slow play topic…..headcovers. These are great for club storage or for travel but have no practical use on the course itself. If you take it off, leave it off until the end of the round. Then there are the totally useless iron covers. We call them iron booties. Golfers that use these on the course generally get some not-so-kind comments. The constant on-an-off of club covers slows play.

Let's talk about the second and subsequent tees. You should play **Ready Golf** on those as well. There is no real need for "Honors". Unless, of course, you want to acknowledge the guy with a birdie. Then please do. Otherwise, hit when you are ready. Remember, if there is a group in front of you, be careful not to hit into them. Let your shorter hitters go first when clear. Then the big guns can let her rip.

I have seen groups where more than one player is using their rangefinder to gauge the distance on a par 3 from the same tee-box. A colossal waste of time. One is enough. Yes, range finders are helpful for those who play regularly. Yet…..do you really need it for every shot?

If you are playing in a group where some are playing the forward tees and those tees are several yards away, try to have those players approach the next tee box ahead of you. They can wait near your tee box until you hit and then move to theirs. That way, they are not waiting for you to walk back to your cart and put your club away before they can even approach their tee.

If anyone hits their drive out-of-bounds, they should tee another up as a provisional. That way if you do not locate the first, you can take the penalty and play the second without having to go back to the tee or take a loss of stroke and distance.

That brings us to that dreaded lost ball. When I have been the Ranger (Marshall) on our course, I found the lost ball situation always caused a backup. If you lose your ball, limit your search to no more than three minutes.

A Snoopy cartoon from Schulz says it best.

Losing a ball is the price you pay. Move on. If you are playing here in the Arizona desert, you may want to forego the search. Let the rattlesnakes rest and the cactus keep their thorns.

Chapter 4 - Fairway play

Now that you have successfully made it off the tee, it's time to see how you can play **Ready Golf** in the Fairway as well.

Please forget what you see the Pros do on television. You are not a Pro, and this is not a million-dollar tournament. There are no cameras, no rules officials, no gallery, and no caddies to consult.

There is a tendency for today's amateurs to play in turn like the Pros. They believe the person farthest away should go first. Bunk! There is no need to wait when you are 20 yards or more apart, not in each other's line and not close enough to bother the other player. Hit when ready! Only wait to hit when you can reach the players in the group ahead.

For example:

Let's assume all players are at their ball after their drive. Who should hit next? Answer: whoever is ready to hit. Player #4 can go whenever he is ready. No one is in his way, and his swing can't affect anyone.

Same with Player #3. Only Player #1 should wait until Player #2 hits.

What if Player #3 and Player #1 are cart mates? Player #1 should drop off Player #3 and then go to his ball. After he hits, Player #3 can walk toward the green and Player#1 can pick him up after he hits.

In cart golf, if you have to walk to your ball away from the cart and your playing partner, take more than one club with you. Do not go to your ball, decide what club you will use, and then go back to the cart to get it. That slows play and frustrates the golfers behind you. Plan ahead.

This is especially true when playing "cart path only". That occurs after overseeding and on especially wet or frost covered ground.

You should not have to rely on another player to give you the yardage. Waiting on them slows play. Time to grow up and get your own device. Odds are you do not have enough control to hit the ball to exact distances anyway.

Just like on the tee, limit the number of practice swings. The only time you may need a couple is when you find yourself in the rough or under a tree.

Which reminds me of another "amateur" fact. Our course used to have pin placements on a sheet for the golfers. They would ask me for "today's" number. I got the biggest kick out of that. Ninety-five percent of them could not hit the ball to that spot anyway. I just told them I just aim for the middle and pray.

We have now gone to red, white, and blue flags like many courses. That is all most amateurs need.

The same **Ready Golf** guidelines used in the fairways apply to approaching and/or being around the green. There is no need to wait for the golfer farthest away to hit first. He/she may be moving the cart or maybe just off the green and trying to decide whether to chip, pitch or putt. Hit when ready.

If you or a playing partner end up in a sand trap, you do not have to wait for everyone to get the green before you hit. It's not an audition for TV.

There will be times when you take more than one club with you around the green. You should lay their clubs out of the way but in a place where they won't be forgotten after you finish the hole.

I always leave my extra club on the edge of the putting green in line with my golf bag or cart. This way the clubs are less likely to be forgotten because I have to walk right over them to get to the next hole. Forgotten clubs can slow your round and can get expensive.

Chapter 5 - On The Green

The green is a hotbed of slow play. I have seen players wait for every golfer to walk onto the green before they approach their ball or even begin to size up their putt. This makes no sense.

If you feel the need to look at your putt from every angle, get it done….and quickly. You can often do this on your way to the green. Many times, this practice is not necessary. The lie does not warrant the TV Pro golfer approach. Two angles are almost always sufficient. This is especially true when you are playing on your "home" course. If you do not know by now how the green breaks, those extra walks around the green won't help you.

Another practice that slows play is marking your golf ball. Why do this if you are not in anyone's line? Sure, you may have to mark, clean and replace. That is the exception. I have seen golfers 30 feet away from the flag walk to the green, mark their ball, and then go back to the cart for their putter. What a waste of time….and energy. If your ball is just off the green, take your putter with you when you chip or pitch. C'mon, people…common sense please.

You may also see that same TV Pro imitation on the green that slows play. That's when someone is waiting for the player to hit who is the farthest out. There is no reason for this. Yes, it may be polite to wait, but that slows play. Hit when ready.

One person in the group may take time to look at his putt from several different angles. If you are ready to go, don't wait for him.

There is also the guy who appears to fall asleep over his putts.

Hopefully, this isn't you.

The recent rule change to allow the pin to remain in has assisted in speeding play. Many golfers are now taking advantage of that. Surprising how many poor putts this has helped. I must admit, I leave it in on the downhill putts.

Game Break: If you want to break 100, you should learn (by practicing) how to lag putt.

That brings me to the "gimme". Everyone has an opinion on this. I believe you should use them if you are playing recreational golf, however, only inside the leather. I am kind of a purist in that regard. It speeds play yet gives one a truer measure of their performance. The beginner may need a bit more encouragement. 😃

If you miss your putt, give serious consideration to putting out. If you choose not to do so, mark only if you are in another's line. Then get out of the way.

After you putt out, tend the flag or pick up the clubs left by others who still have to putt. That speeds play.

Another contributor to slow play is marking the scorecards on the green. Wait until you get to the next tee.

Always fix your ball mark as soon as you reach the green. If you find you must wait on another player to putt, fix another ball mark. I make it a practice to fix at least one more than mine.

Now you and your group have played **Ready Golf.** You have completed the round in just under four hours. It is time to leave the 18th green, return the carts, and head to the 19th hole. That is the best place to compute the scores, settle the bets, and talk about what was or could have been.

In the event you are not familiar with the "19th hole" reference, I will explain. This is slang for a restaurant, pub, grill, or course clubhouse. That is where many golfers go at the end of their round for refreshments and chitchat.

Chapter 6 - Etiquette Matters

Do's & Don'ts

These may not always be contributors to slow play, but they can most certainly impact the pleasure of the game for those involved.

Do's

- Play **Ready Golf**

- Respect the course and fill divots.

- Repair ball marks on greens.

- Stay fully on the cart paths around tees and greens. No one is coming to pass you.

- Follow instructions of the Ranger (Marshall) on duty.

- Adhere to cart path signs.

- Follow pace of play guidelines set by the course.

- Take your trash with you when you leave the course.

- Tip the Starter. (Just kidding… us old farts just do this so we can play free golf)

- Respect the property of homeowners next to the course. It's not a public right-of-way.

Don'ts:

- Talk, make noise, or walk around during another's stroke.

- Walk in another player's line on the green. For beginners, that is the path their ball may take to the hole.

- Stand behind a player while they putt.

- Ever offer advice on another person's play unless specifically asked to do so. This is a cardinal sin.

- Pick up another player's ball unless he has finished the hole.

- Drive off the cart path onto the grass around tees and greens. Keep all four wheels on the path.

- Hit into players in front of you. If you do so by accident, yell "Fore" loud enough for them to hear. Then apologize.

- Litter the course. Take out what you bring in.

Epilog

I truly hope you now understand what is meant by **Ready Golf.** I hope you found this educational. If you are already a proponent, I hope you found it entertaining. Perhaps it may serve as a gift….a nudge for someone that is not so enlightened.

Writing it did help me "get it off my chest".

May God be with you and help you enjoy the blessings a day in the grass can bring.

"Trust in the Lord with all your heart and lean not on your own understanding; in all ways acknowledge Him and He will make your path straight!"

-Proverbs 3:5-6 (NIV)

Bonus Section

Let's talk about equipment. The game of golf can get expensive. This is especially true if you try to always have the latest and greatest thing to hit the market. Golfers tend to change equipment frequently. They believe it will improve their game. Actually, lessons would be a better investment. I know that from experience.

The majority of the major club manufacturers are designing clubs to fit the golf professionals, not amateurs. The bigger headed drivers are not always the easiest to hit. So, start out with older, less expensive models. You'll find most golf and sports equipment outlets have a plethora of quality used clubs.

Club shafts also come in many different compositions. It's almost like flavors of ice cream in a Baskin-Robins. Most golf equipment outlets will let you try out clubs right in the store. They will also help you select ones that fit you. They can also tell you what your swing speed is.

Another key piece of equipment is the ball itself. Here again, there are more options than you can grasp. Most golfers try to mimic the Pros and choose the same brand of ball.

More important than brand is compression. I found a web site that lists the compression of most golf balls and includes the swing speed suitedfor that ball. https://golfguidebook.com/golf-ball-compression-chart/

My advice for your next round of golf:

"Hit it long and straight, just not often."

www.ingramcontent.com/pod-product-compliance
Lightning Source LLC
Chambersburg PA
CBHW041228050726

47599CB00001B/113